Every Child's Money Survival Kit

First published 2008
Second edition 2017
Third edition 2020
Copyright© Christine Thompson-Wells 2008
All rights reserved
No production without the prior permission of the publisher
No part of this book, including interior design, cover design, illustrations and icons may be
reproduced or transmitted in any form, by any means
(electronic, photocopying, recording or otherwise) without the prior
permission of the publisher and author

ISBN: 978-0-6480836-6-5

Published by Books For Reading On Line.Com

See our web site: *www.booksforreadingonline.com*

Or contact by email:

sales@booksforreadingonline.com

Australia

Charities

There are many charities that need financial support and help to continue their work. Therefore, we donate 10% of the net sales of each book to a charity. The charities include: cancer research, diabetes type one, children's hospitals, mental health support and other aid organisations.

Will Jones Space Adventures
&
The Zadrilian Queen
Created for children
Will Jones

To assist with Financial Intelligence through education

Concept Education

$C_{oncept} + E_{ducation} = L_{earning}$

Resource Pack

Testimonials

Will Jones' Space Adventures & The Zadrilian Queen

'This is an exciting novel that can be used by children in so many different ways. Primarily, the book can be as a fun, exciting book that allows children to think and work with a money system, they may think:

- How much money do I have?
- How do I spend and save money?
- When do I use a helmet when cycling and what are the consequences of not using one?

- Maintaining and looking after things – Will's bike is fixed by a member of the Grigan race from the Planet of Grigan.
- Family values, rules and ethics.
- Will learnt such great lessons on the Planet of Zadril.

Lovely ending; makes you want to read the next book.'

Liz Pennell, Teacher and Mother.

'I found the book easy to understand. The illustrations are very good and the chapters aren't too long. I found the money side to the story very interesting. I would recommend this book to my friends and family and my school.

Charlotte Sloper, Student.

The Next Will Jones' Book - Will Jones' Space Adventures &
The Children of the Black Sun – A chilling story.

Also, don't forget about Will Jones' Space Adventures & The Money Formula.

Money School

Brief for teachers, home educators, community group & holiday programme leaders and others

How to use this Resource Pack

The products developed at Money School are tested by teachers and children in the classroom, homes and working with families, working or teaching community groups, school, teacher and parent groups.

Used by the media such as Th Times Education Supplement and other forms of media.

It is our aim to make learning essential life-skills: working with and managing money, as easy and exciting as possible. We could not do this if our products were not thoroughly trialled under many different conditions.

The Objectives:

1. To allow children to learn through the activities of reading, acting and song how to work and understand the concept of money.
2. To allow the children to learn through working on parchments (worksheets) and puzzles how the concept of money will affect them in their real life environment.
3. To help the child develop life skills before they are faced with money issues or problems.

Will Jones' Space Adventures & The Zadrilian Queen is an adventurous book that is suitable for children from about 6 years through to young adults of 14 and older. In fact, because the story is so good, this book has been recommended for teenagers, parents and grandparents.

'This book could ideally be used in cross-curricula subjects: PSHE, Math, Drama, Financial Education, Citizenship, Mime Activities, Assemblies, Art, RE, English, Science and Topic Work.' Liz Pennell.

Will Jones' Space Adventures and The Zadrilian Queen takes the reader on an adventure that is not only about working with and managing money but on how ethics, morality, values and accountability work within our communities. If children are not taught how to work ethically whole civilisations, in the future, may suffer. Entwine ethics, morality, values and accountability with this space adventure and there is a winner for enthusiastic learning.

To read the book for the adventure alone is a rewarding experience but if it is used in conjunction with the Resource Pack and the Play then the benefits to the child become triple fold.

Will Jones' Space Adventures and The Money Formula book teach children how to work a simple formula: to work with and manage money. By using the formula, a child may look forward to a life of financial self-sustainability, well-being and satisfaction.

Will Jones' Space Adventures and The Zadrilian Queen take the reader to a higher level of thinking about money and gives a lateral approach to money and its' principles. For educators: the Will Jones' series are written and designed to work through cognitive stimulation – simply, creating fun in learning. When principles of learning are learned in a non-threatening environment, the child/learner easily holds onto the learned information. They, in turn, build mental hooks that more and more information can be hooked to. With these 'right' conditions in learning, a child can become an insatiable learner and in turn develop life-skills that will keep him/her financially safe.

Will Jones' Space Adventures and The Zadrilian Queen – The Book

Like all of the Will Jones' books, this book comes in two versions: The Schools version is shortened and is designed to give the essential story and contains about 10,500 words. This version, at the beginning of each chapter: Pause and Pay Attention allowing the child to make deliberate stopping points within the chapter; this stopping allows the child to take the time to reinforce the learned information. At the end of the chapter, they are asked to 'Recap.'

We suggest that each child takes a chapter at a time and completes the Question Sheet at the back of each chapter. The chapters are concise each building an exciting story as the reader travels their journey. The stories are intertwined. As Will's adventure continues, Princess Eex shows her determination in all that she does – she creates a positive role model. Her mother, The Queen of Zadril also shows the same determination and is very much an action person. Will, again, is the facilitator in the story – he keeps the stories going through his sense of adventure; his insatiable appetite for learning are all woven into the values he has as a young adult.

The high street version takes the reader deeply into the story and is a standalone story book which contains about 29,500 words.

Will Jones' Space Adventures and The Zadrilian Queen – The Play

The Play consists of seven, twenty-minute scenes. Once the book is read, the Play makes for positive reinforcement to the story of Will Jones, his values, morality, and ethics. The Play also stimulates group work and interaction – children of varied capabilities can feel comfortable, but still keep learning an essential life-skill of managing money through the interaction that takes place during rehearsals and performance.

Extra curricula activities may also be built into the fun of learning of money through creating stage props as projects and the activities of the preparation of costumes: crowns, cardboard coins, green geometric shapes and more.

Will Jones' Space Adventures and The Zadrilian Queen – Resource Pack

This pack comes with nine worksheets (parchments) and answer sheets. You have a choice of using black and white or coloured copies. The child/children may choose to colour in the black and white copies. Also contained in the pack are two Zadrilian Awards. An Award is given to the child/children at the teacher's discretion. The discretion may be when a child has completed the reading book, parchments or play. We do stress, giving the Award too easily will lessen the value of the work done. The child/children should feel he or she has earned the right to the Award.

Please note: Will Jones' Space Adventures & The Zadrilian Queen – The Play and Resource Pack are optional extras and are bought separately.

Will Jones' Space Adventures and The Zadrilian Queen - Lesson Plan – The Supermarket of Zadril

The Lesson Plan has been developed to assist teachers and educators in delivering the Will Jones' package. The lesson plan will help teachers to set up the Zadrilian Supermarket on the Planet of Zadril.

The supermarket of Zadril has been designed to extend children through preparation for their working life.

The first section of the exercise contains six buying sources that allow Mr & Mrs Pleant to buy from to stock their supermarket. These are: The Dairy Farmer, The Crop Farmer, The Fruit and Vegetable Farmer, The Chicken Farmer, The Fishermen, and the Warehouse.

The roles are distinctive while the children are in the action of the play but the roles should be alternated so that all children experience the different approaches to different working environments.

Contained within the guidelines for running the programme are a number of charts that assist the children in bringing together the actual workings of a supermarket. In these charts the children are encouraged to work out from the wholesale price, the retail price by adding percentages.

The project will need to be built from the beginning and the children should be encouraged to bring to school clean, used, empty containers that contribute to goods or stock contained within a warehouse or supermarket. These are later used for selling at the supermarket.

The Aim of Will Jones' Space Adventures & The Zadrilian Queen

Is to give children a base understanding and to allow them to know what money is, where it comes from, how money is used, where money goes, how to look after money, how to spend and budget money and how money works in the wider world.

The Objective of Will Jones' Space Adventures & The Zadrilian Queen

Is to allow children to learn through the activities of: reading, acting, song, working on parchments (worksheets) and puzzles how the concept of money will effect them in their real life environment.

The Will Jones' Space Adventures' book will assist the teacher to cover the objectives:

Recognise the difference in coins and notes; introduce children to different coins (euros and other countries currency can be introduced here); understand that, in some instances, change may be given. The Will Jones' & the Zadrilian Queen book will assist with this objective; recognise there is a difference between earned money and gift money (pocket money). Allow children to realise there is a difference between the things they want and the things they need. Allow the children to recognise that there are other expenses (Ziob, will help you to cover this topic). The children will start to understand how giving will help other people less fortunate than themselves. By saving carefully and staying in control of their money they will ensure well-being in the future. *(The Will Jones' Money Formula will assist all children to manage their money.)* Children will start to understand that responsibility needs to be taken for the things they buy.

It is important to remember, that money is a concept and that each child and family will see the value of money from a different perspective: – some families have enough, some have too little and some have a lot of money. Each child will come from a different environment. In some households, money is never spoken of and in some other households money is always a topical issue. In some households there may not be enough money to pay the bills or perhaps, the parents (in another household) may be looking at the next investment portfolio they are planning to buy? It may also be, that some families are struggling with unmanageable debt – sensitivity is needed with all of these points.

Experience has taught me that money is a sensitive area to teach.

Where are the children going in the 21st century?

Over a period of twelve months we undertook research in five schools in the Berkshire and Surrey areas. We wanted to test the hypothesis:

> *'Children who develop a money skill at an early age show an immediate awareness of responsibility for working with and managing their money.'*

Seventy-three children, Head Teachers, teachers, parents, and other people took part in the investigation.

Our hypothesis proved to be positive and that children do like to know where they are going with their money and how to work with a money system.

Brief overview:

As a teacher, businesswoman, educator and mother I have written the Will Jones' series of books (there are eight in all) for children. There is a need for all children worldwide to learn the life-skill of managing money. Money education now is more important than in 2,500 years of past civilisations working with coinage as a means of currency. The currency systems of the world are now changing into 'cashless' societies. Adding to this knowledge was the prompt that came after my observations in the classroom and watching children trying to balance their daily and weekly money and observing some of the struggles they went through not to mention here, my own experiences, observation and qualitative research that took place when the people in our community experienced a recession that was brought on through a change in national government.

As chairperson of a curriculum advisory committee for three years, teacher at the University of Canberra; teacher at colleges and schools, teaching young offenders in young offender institutions, head of psychology at a girls' school, author and a university education within a Faculty of Education of nearly twelve years, I have gained an in-depth working knowledge to curriculum and its aims and objectives. I was also invited on to a steering group by the Department of Children, Schools & Families (DCSF) UK to participate in the Financial Capability objectives for 2009. The Will Jones' series is written with the curriculum used as a 'back-bone' to all the stories – the child is learning but does not realise they are learning life-skills. They are learning money management life-skills through fun and adventure.

One child can save and look after his/her money, while another child in the same family, spends every coin or note he/she has either earned or has been given. The concept and perception of money is different with every individual.

I ask why is this so? When I was at school, we had the classroom mock up shop where we had limited goods to buy and sell and as I recall, the exercise gave to us children very little in return. That is not to say that the teachers did not try hard to do their best; they did.

As a mature adult with over thirty years in education and business, I have again looked at the scenario of 'Why some people struggle with money management and why some do not?' This question, together with my research, has led me to develop this series of space adventure books for children and adults. My aim is to make this learning a fun thing to do for everybody.

There are more books on their way.

Rupins and shapes are fictitious currencies that are used in Will Jones' Space Adventure stories. Will lives on the fictitious island of Ozimoth. He has a conventional home and school life, which allows almost all children to identify with him. The fictitious planets and space people allow the young reader to have the story time that we all love as children while learning about a crucial development in growing up. That is staying in control of our money and life situations.

I believe, in this age of awareness to young peoples' 'needs', that we have to work more and more with the multiple intelligence approach to each, and every child in every aspect of education.

As a teacher of psychology, I know how important it is to create the positive mental pathways in the mind that will lead to positive and constructive, non-threatening outcomes for the child and older student – a child or older person in fear will never learn! Once the negative mental barriers are in place it is very difficult to knock them down!

The development of the series of books is to progress and develop this idea so that teachers, parents, brothers and sisters, grandparents and all of us who want to continue learning and, of course, the young learner, may enjoy the challenge of learning a complex and challenging monetary system. They will then, be able to use the knowledge they gain to their advantage and that, in turn, will make them pro-active, confident adults.

As I have previously said, we are rapidly progressing into a cashless society. Our children and grandchildren will not be as fortunate as we have been – we have had the privilege of using and working with money in the mechanical sense. We can pick up a cent, penny, yen, euro, dollar, pound or note — in a cashless society this does not happen. We have therefore been privileged to work the mechanical processes with our eyes, touch, smell, and the jingle of change in our pockets and purses. These experiences create some of the necessary pathways in our minds that allow us to develop our money management techniques and knowledge. Future generations will possibly not have this privilege; they may only see a bank statement and a plastic card!

If we give the young student the mental tools at least he/she will be able to choose the way they want to operate their money system.

Supermarket Zadril

Lesson Plan

It is important to remember: During this exercise the children will be introduced to two forms of currency: Rupins and Pennies from the Island of Ozimoth and Shapes and Parts from the Planet of Zadril; both currencies work with the decimal system of 100

Within the supermarket on Zadril there are six main areas that the owners (Mr & Mrs Pleant) of the supermarket buys from:

1) Buying the produce to sell to their customers from the dairy farmer.

2) Buying the products to sell to their customers from the crop farmer, who makes his own bread and cakes.

3) Buying the produce to sell to their customers from the vegetable and fruit farmer.

4) Buying from the chicken farmer to sell to their customers.

5) Buying fresh fish from the fisherman to sell to their customers.

6) Buying the goods to re-sell to their customers from the warehouse.

The dairy farmer produces from his cows, milk, cream, yoghurt, icen cream and cheese to re-sell at the supermarket.

The crop farmer grows grain and from the grain and makes bread, cakes, buns, biscuits, bagels, rolls and oats for porridge to re-sell at the supermarket.

The Fruit and Vegetable farmer The Supermarket of Zadril normally buys its fresh apples, plums, potatoes, cauliflower, beetroot, some tomatoes from the fruit and vegetable farmer

The chicken farmer – The teacher may like to explain about the 'chicken and egg scenario here. When the chickens are the right age, they are then killed so that their meat can be sold to the customers, who do their shopping, at the supermarket.

The fisherman – The fisherman goes out daily to catch fish from the sea. He too, sells his fish to Mr & Mrs Pleant so that they can re-sell it to their customers.

BUYING GOODS AT THE WAREHOUSE

The warehouse – the warehouse is run by a manager or the owner.
Explain to the children that a manager is the person (it can be a woman or man) that makes sure that the warehouse always has enough products or produce to sell to the supermarket. He or she needs to know who is buying what at what time so that products, (if they run out) can be re-ordered in a hurry. Explain: Christmas Time, special holidays and festive times, the warehouse may run out of products if they do not buy enough from their own suppliers.

Supermarket owners go to the warehouse to buy the products they need to put on the shelves of their shops so that their customers can see what is for sale. The supermarket sells a number of different goods. Some of the goods are: detergent that we use when we wash up the dishes; we also put clothes washing detergent into the washing machine when we wash our clothes. The supermarket sells tomato sauce used when we cook, and sometimes we put tomato sauce into bolognaise or use tomato sauce to pour over hot potato chips. The supermarket also sells toilet rolls to use in the bathroom and rice brought in from other countries. All of these products are sold at the warehouse. (A teacher may add more and more products.)

Explain: to the children, each of these people: the dairy farmer, the crop farmer, the fruit and vegetable farmer, the chicken farmer, the fisherman and the warehouse manager must be paid for providing the products and goods to Mr & Mrs Pleant. The milk and dairy products from the dairy farmer, cakes and biscuits from the crop farmer, the fruit and vegetable farmer, chicken farmer and fish from the fisherman, also, the detergents, toilet rolls and household goods from the Manager at the warehouse.

Explain: All of these people (the people who provide goods and products to be sold in the supermarket are called suppliers.)

From the money that Mr & Mrs Pleant pay to the suppliers, the suppliers also have to pay their own expenses. The dairy farmer will need to pay for feed to feed the animals and to the vet for keeping his animals healthy. The farmer will also need to buy new animals when his herd becomes too old to produce milk. The fisherman would have to pay for his boat and the petrol it takes the boat to go out to sea. The manager of the warehouse has to pay the suppliers who supply the detergents, the toilet rolls, tomato sauce and the other goods you find in the supermarket. For instance: tomato sauce, toilet rolls, and other products are usually made by the manufacturers in a factory somewhere on the Planet of Zadril

Ask: 'What would you expect to buy at a supermarket?'

Wait for answer, gives some prompts. Remind the children about a visit to the supermarket they have made recently and what did they or their parents pay for?

Ask: Once you have an answer, 'Do you understand, and would anybody like to talk about the food we eat or does anybody know anybody who owns or works in a supermarket?'

The Project

To Build the Supermarket on the Planet of Zadril: – Encourage the children to bring to school old but clean: yoghurt, butter, egg, ice cream, drink containers, breakfast cereal boxes and general packaging that could be used in the shop.

Building the project may take two or more lessons. You will need to collect your stock before opening your supermarket. Children can make cardboard loaves of bread, cakes, pies and biscuits. Many of these shapes can be downloaded from the internet or they can be drawn freehand. We have added some clip art to get you started.

     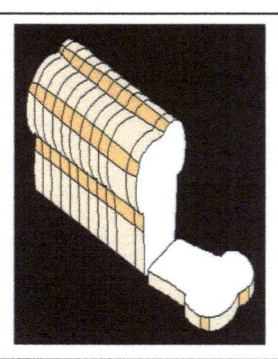

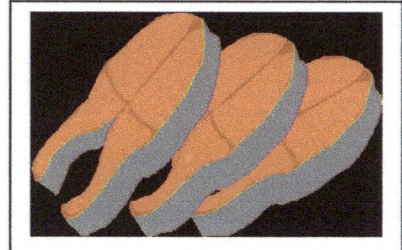 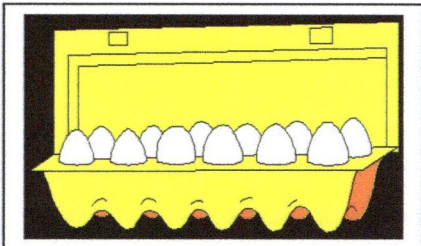  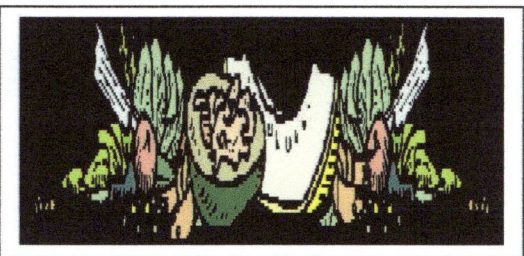

Responsibility should be given to every child to bring into the group used containers. Optional: the containers can be sold to the wholesale manager for cash.

Explain: A supermarket is a business. All businesses have to make money. Once Mr & Mrs Pleant have bought their produce, products and goods they will need to sell them. They cannot sell them for the same price that they bought them for from the suppliers; they must sell them at a higher price than what they bought them for.

For the exercise only, we will charge 10% extra on everything that is sold at the Supermarket on Zadril. Supermarket owners may charge more or less but we will keep to the 10% to allow the children to follow the programme.

Ozimoth Money

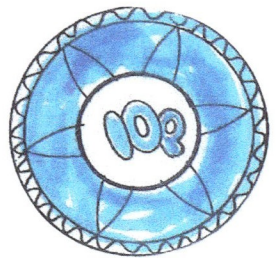

Will, explains, 'There are 100 Pennies to a Rupin R. We have Rupins in paper money and coins on the Island of Ozimoth!'

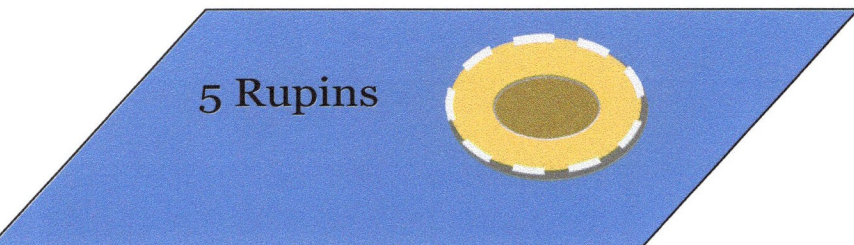

A good idea is to also introduce your national currency at this point. Relating the real money to pretend money gives the necessary mental links that allows for understanding the **value** when exchanging money for goods and services.

Zadrilian Money

While sitting on the floor in the Palace of Zadril, Will and the group are very excited as they all start to talk about money and how it works. Will continues to explain: '...your money has different names but still works in decimals. For instance,' he stops in the middle of the sentence while he thinks and scratches his head, he suddenly realises in amazement, then continues, '...your Shape is 100 Parts, the same as our Rupin is 100 Pennies and one Part is one Part of a hundred, the same as our Penny is one part of a hundred!' The Butler explains excitedly, 'Yes, Yes, you are right Will, you are right – that is so exciting!'

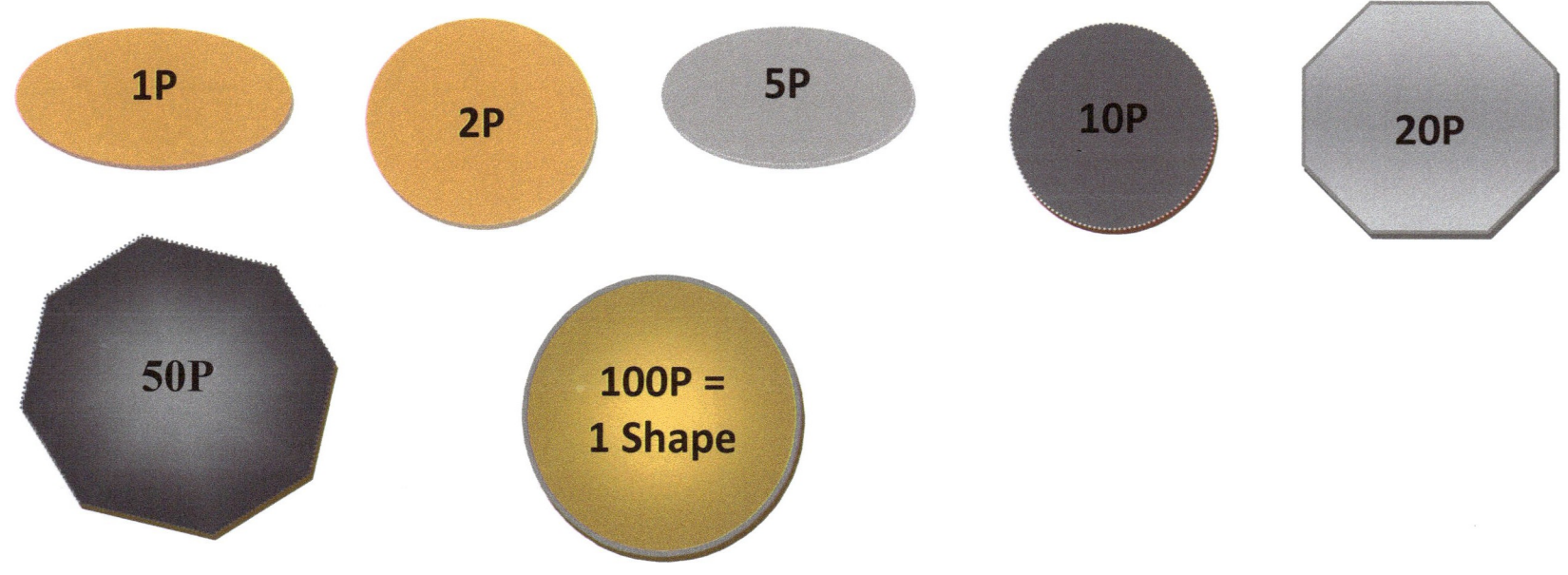

The Lesson

The Farmers, the Wholesale Manager at the Warehouse, Mr & Mrs Pleant, the owners of the Zadril supermarket and the customers will need to be selected.
So select:

- The Dairy Farmer
- The Crop Farmer
- The Fruit and Vegetable Farmer
- The Chicken Farmer
- The Fresh Fish Fisherman
- Mr & Mrs Pleant – the Supermarket Zadril owners.

The remainder of the class may be employed by the farmers to do odd jobs around the farms. Some of the children may need to be employed by Mr & Mrs Pleant to help them to run the supermarket, to stack the shelves and work on the checkout. Some children may be employed by the Warehouse Manager to help him/her with the orders they receive. Some of the children will need to be the customers of the supermarket.

The farmers will need to prepare their products for sale to the supermarket. Mr & Mrs Pleant will add their 10% so the price that the farmer charges the supermarket owners will not be the same price that the customers buy the produce or product for. A farmer for example, will sell his loaf of bread at 10 Pennies, if the supermarket owners then put on their mark-up of 10% which is 1 penny; this makes a selling or the retail price for the loaf of bread 11 pennies. An example of a worksheet follows.

Exercise In Adding 10%

Prices of the products & produce that Mr & Mrs Pleant will sell in their supermarket	Mr & Mrs Pleant Add 10%	Retail price or cost to customer
1 loaf of bread 10 Parts	1 Part	11 Parts
6 eggs 60 Parts	6 Parts	66 Parts
3 cup cakes at 10 Parts each = 30 Parts	3 Parts	33 Parts
1 block of cheese 1 Shape and 60 Parts	16 Parts	1 Shape and 76 Parts or S1.76P
1 birthday cake 6 Shape and 80 Parts	68 Parts	7 Shapes and 80 Parts or S 7.80

Cut out and photocopy the following chart (You will need enough copies – one for each child) and use it to get the children started on the project. A second chart is provided (without products, produce or goods) you may copy and cut this chart out ready for the role-play. This chart may also be used when the children bring in their own containers, boxes etc for sale in the shop.

> Children's Chart of Prices
> Encourage the children to work out the 10% added to the product/produce/goods and then the retail price

Prices of the products & produce that Mr & Mrs Pleant will sell in their supermarket	Mr & Mrs Pleant Add 10% (Fill in 10%)	Retail Price or Cost to Customer
1 box of cereal at 1 Shape and 60 Parts		
1 chicken at 3 Shapes and 50 Parts		
1 cup cake at 10 Parts		
1 container of ice cream at 2 Shapes and 30 Parts		
1 dozen eggs at 1 Shape and 20 Parts		

> The Price List –
> Choose a product from the clip art and give it a wholesale price. Allow the children to work out the percentages and the selling or retail prices.

Prices of the products & produce that Mr & Mrs Pleant will sell in their supermarket	Mr & Mrs Pleant Add 10% (Fill in 10%)	Retail Price or Cost to Customer
Product for sale	10% extra	How much will the customer pay?
Product for sale	10% extra	How much will the customer pay?
Product for sale	10% extra	How much will the customer pay?
Product for sale	10% extra	How much will the customer pay?
Product for sale	10% extra	How much will the customer pay?

Once the children have worked out the selling/retail price, they can then fill in the name of the product/produce/good on the pricing labels provided.

(We suggest that you copy many copies of these)

Example of Pricing Labels

Price
Block of Cheese
S1 60 Parts

Price
Birthday Cakes
S6 80 Parts
Each

Price
Cup Cakes
10 Parts
Each

Price
Loaf of Bread
10 Parts
Each

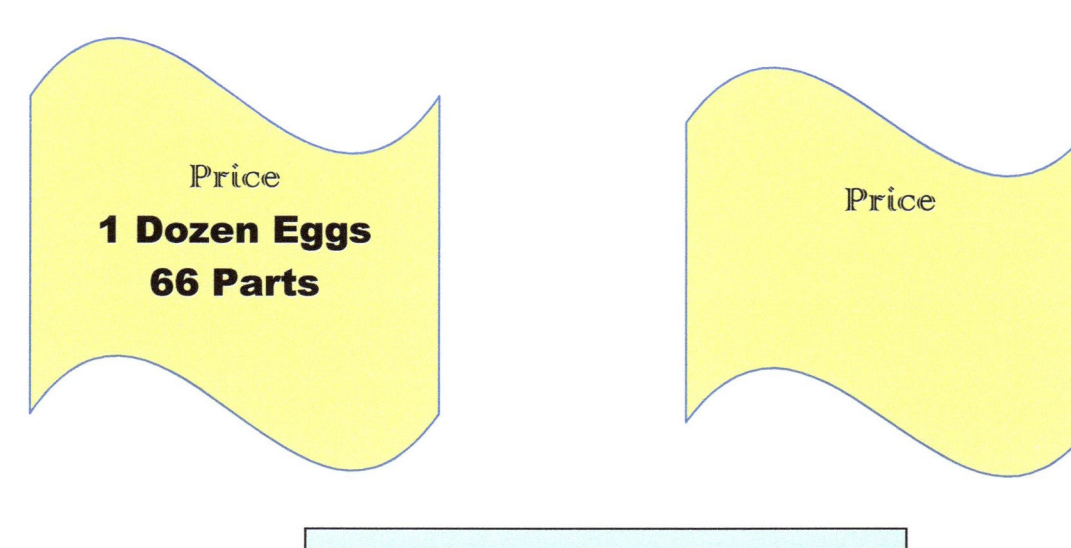

Your Pricing Labels (Copy More)

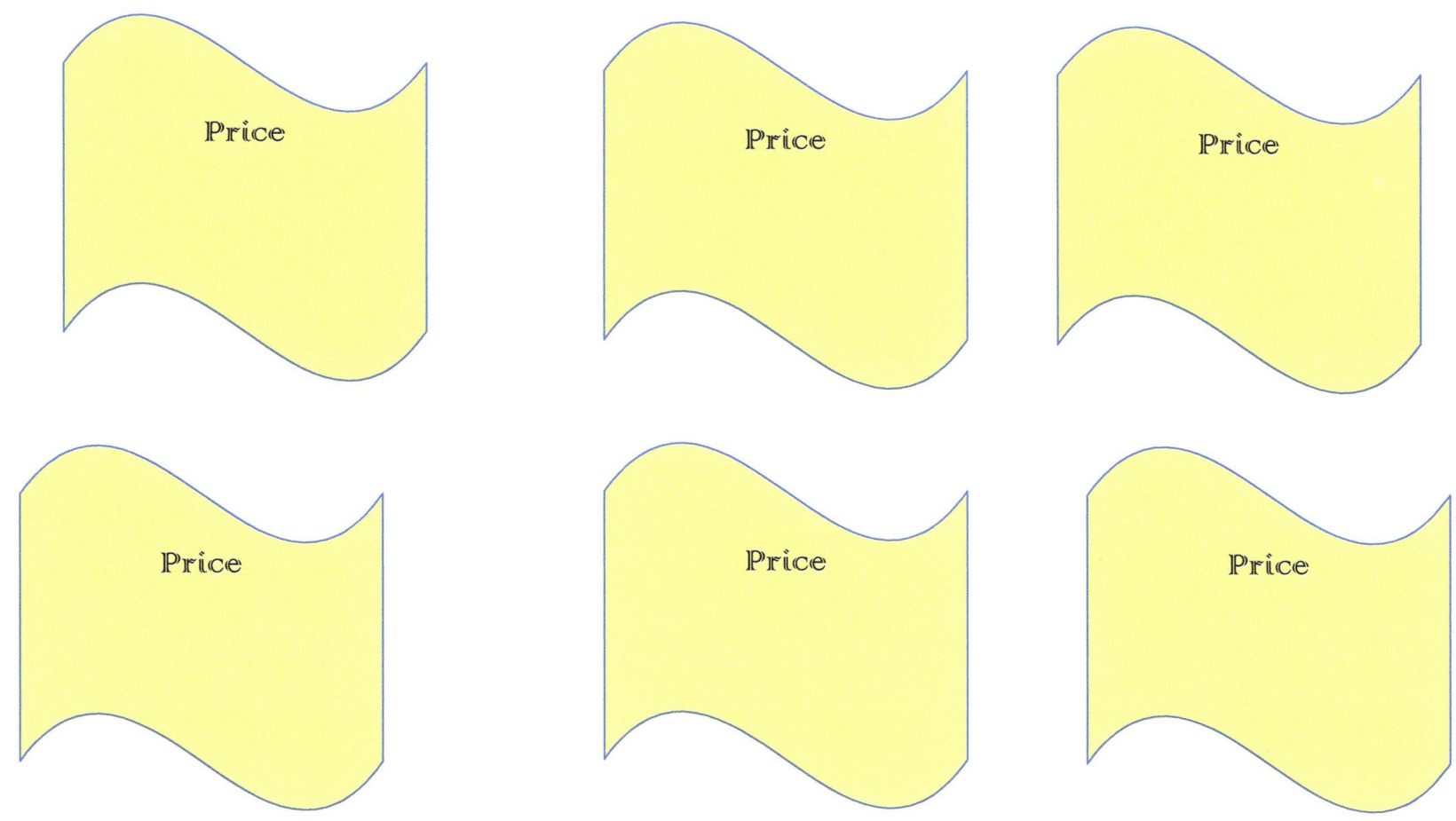

Selling Produce, Products and Goods for the Supermarket

Once all of the stock is prepared that means, collected, priced, labelled and ready for resale, the children will need to have a place to sell and buy their goods.

Setting up the farms, warehouse and shop are important tasks and will add to the success of the project.

All of the children must feel that have an important role to play. If you like, running a business and working with money, though money is a concept, the money always needs to be run as a system – it must have a beginning, middle and end process. Children will need to know, that people need to earn money. They will need to know: where the goods/stock are coming from, how much it costs at the wholesale price from the warehouse, how much the farmer charged and how much Mr & Mrs Pleant are charging (the retail price) in their super market? They will need to see the difference.

The children will also need to keep time sheets of how long they are working (please see the time sheet below.) They might be working for one of the farmers or for Mr & Mrs Pleant or at the warehouse. If you have read Will Jones' Space Adventures & The Zadrilian Queen, you would have seen Will's Time Sheet, from the farmer on Ozimoth. He unfolds the time sheet while speaking to the Queen of Zadril, Princess Eex, Little Brother and the Elderly Zadrilian Butler. We have developed another Time Sheet that you can copy and use in this programme.

During the role-play, we suggest that the children work for 30 minutes in each selected group. For instance: Mr & Mrs Pleant will employ people to work at the check out and some will be employed to stack the shelves of the supermarket. After 30 minutes, the roles should change. The children working in the supermarket may need to work for one of the farmer's and one of the farmer's may need to work in the warehouse and so on.

How to fill in the Time Sheets should be explained to the children.

Explain: When people go to work, they are paid for the hours they work – this is why we keep Time Sheets. People do not keep Time Sheets in all jobs. For instance, doctors, teachers, and other people do not always keep a Time Sheet. Nurses keep records of the hours they work and so do lorry or truck drivers. For this exercise, you are going to keep a Time Sheet just to see how long it takes to do the jobs you are given. You can talk about the Time Sheet after and during the project.

The Time Sheets
Copy More

TIME SHEET

NAME:..

TIME START	TIME FINISHED	TIME WORKED	RATE OF PAY PER HOUR	PAYMENT DUE
MONDAY				
TUESDAY				
WEDNESDAY				
THURSDAY				
FRIDAY				

Children should be encouraged to keep a record of the hours they work for each employer during the role-play. Other areas that records should be kept are in the purchase of goods from:

- **Sales of goods from the farmers to the supermarket**
- **Sales of goods from the warehouse to the supermarket**
- **Sales of goods made at the supermarket by the customers.**

RECORD SHEETS OF GOODS BOUGHT AND SOLD COPY MORE

SALE OF GOODS	NUMBER SOLD	PRICE	TOTAL
CHEESE			
BIRTHDAY CAKE/S			
CEREAL			
CUP CAKE/S			
BEANS			
BREAD			
CHICKEN			
FRUIT			
HAMBURGER			
FISH			
GINGER CAKE			
ICE CREAM			
TOTAL:			

It is ideal to run the lessons over three to four weeks. By doing this, each child becomes familiar with the process of the supermarket, where the goods, products and produce come from and how they are bought and sold.

At the end of the programme we have designed a questionnaire that can be given out to every child. The questionnaire will guide you and the effectiveness of the programme.

Supermarket Zadril – Questionnaire
Please answer the questions below and return to your teacher.

Questionnaire

1) Did you enjoy the role-play at the Supermarket on Zadril?
   (Yes)   (No)

2) Would you like to do the role-play again?
   (Yes)   (No)

3) Did you learn how the owners of the Supermarket on Zadril buy its produce from the Dairy Farmer?
   (Yes)   (No)

4) Do you understand why the owners of the Supermarket have to put 10% onto the cost of the produce they buy from the farmer
   (Yes)   (No)

4) Do you understand that the warehouse has different products to the farmers to sell to the Supermarket?
   (Yes)   (No)

5) What does the Crop Farmer sell to the Supermarket: Please tick: (Fish) (Milk) (Cereal) (Burgers?)

6) What does the Dairy Farmer sell to the Supermarket: Please tick: (Eggs) (Detergent) (Custard) (Milk?)

Thank you for completing this questionnaire.

Lots of XANNNTS
Say and count the Xannnts' legs as you work

Parchment 1

GETTING YOU STARTED

Xannnts have eight legs

Fill in the number in the blank coloured space.
See how quickly you can count the legs of the Xannnts.

1)

2)

| 2 lots of eight | | |
| 8 + 8 = | 16 | legs |

| 3 lots of eight | | |
| 8 + 8 + 8 = | | legs |

3)

4)  (5 crabs)

| 4 lots of eight | | |
| 8 + 8 + 8 + 8 = | | legs |

| 5 lots of eight | | |
| 8 + 8 + 8 + 8 + 8 = | | legs |

5)

6)

| 7 lots of eight | | |
| 8 + 8 + 8 + 8 + 8 + 8 + 8 = | | legs |

| 6 lots of eight | | |
| 8 + 8 + 8 + 8 + 8 + 8 + = | | legs |

There's a tricky question here, so watch your answer!

MORE LOTS OF
Say and count the coins as you work

Parchment 2

1p is equal to 1 Part of a hundred

5p is 5 parts of a hundred
5 X 1 = 5P
5 lots of 1P = 5P

This coin is 5P or 5 Parts

We have 5 lots of 5 Parts here.
That means we have 25 Parts of a hundred.
5 coins X 5 Parts = 25P

This coin is 2p or 2 parts of a hundred

We have 5 lots of 2 Parts here.
That means we have 10 Parts of a hundred.
5 coins X 2 Parts = 10 Parts

This coin is 10P or 10 Parts

We have 5 lots of 10 Parts here.
That means we have 50 Parts of a hundred.
5 coins X 10 Parts = 50P

Q 1) How many lots of 1P do you have?

Q 2) How many lots of 10P do you have? And how much does it come to?

Q 3) How many Parts do you have altogether? And how much does it come to?

A 1)

A 2)

A 3)

Buying And Selling

Parchment 3

Q 1)

Each Xannnt will cost you 15P.
How much will 4 cost?

Answer Box

Q 2) You have 6 Xannnts and want to sell them for 20P each. How much will you get if you sell them all?

Answer Box

Q 5)

Q 3)

You have 7 Xannnts and you want to sell 4 of them.
You will charge 17P each.
How much money will you get if you sell the 4 Xannts?

Answer Box

Q 4) You want to buy a King Xannnt that costs 70P and you have 1 Shape in your pocket. If you buy the King Xannnt how much will you have left?

Answer Box

You have paid 15P each for your Xannnts. You bought 4. Now you now want to sell them for 20P each.
1) How much did you pay for the Xannnts?
2) How much will you sell your Xannnts for?
3) If you sell them all, how much profit will you make?

Buying Things!

Parchment 4

Choose the coins you need to buy the things then draw the coins in the box

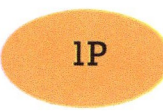 1P
 2P
 5P
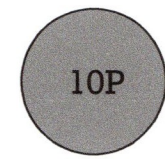 10P
 20P
 50P
 1 Shape

| 1P = 1 Par | 2P = 2 Parts | 5P = 5 Parts | 10P = 10 Parts | 20P = 20 Parts | 50P = 50 Parts | 100p = 100 Parts or 1 Shape |

| Drum 75P | Ball 45P | Doll 95P | Lunar cart S1.35P | Skateboard S1.50P |

 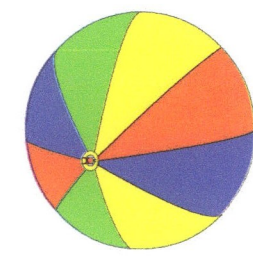   

Parchment 5

Link the amounts and write the total –

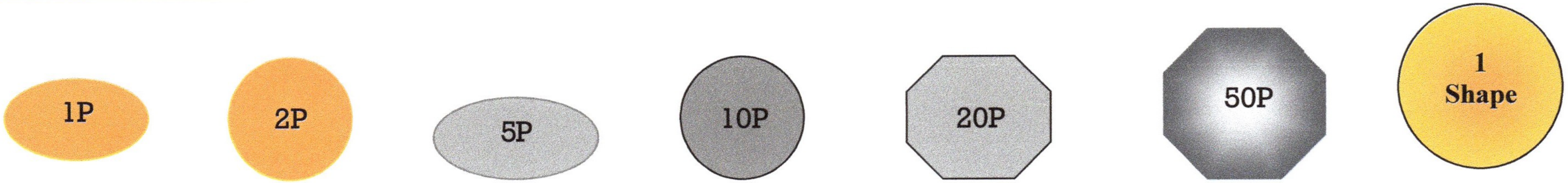

orange oval	1P
orange circle	2P
grey oval	5P
dark grey circle	10P
light grey octagon	20P
dark grey octagon	50P
yellow circle	1 Shape

- 1P = 1 Part
- 2P = 2 Parts
- 5P = 5 Parts
- 10P = 10 Parts
- 20P = 20 Parts
- 50P = 50 Parts
- 100P = 100 Parts

1) 10P, 20P, 10P — TOTAL:

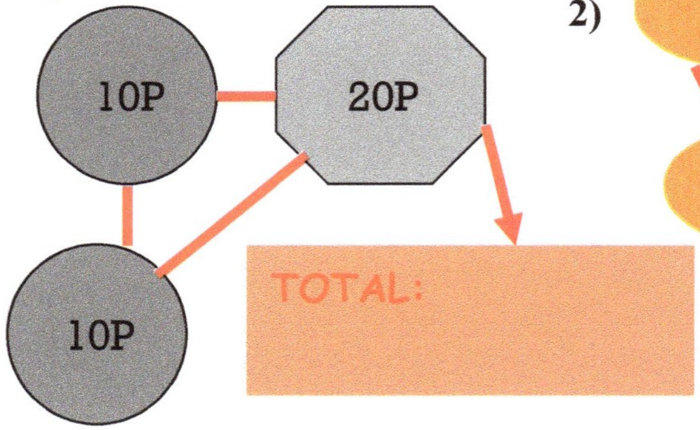

2) 1P, 1P, 1P, 1P, 1P, 20P — TOTAL:

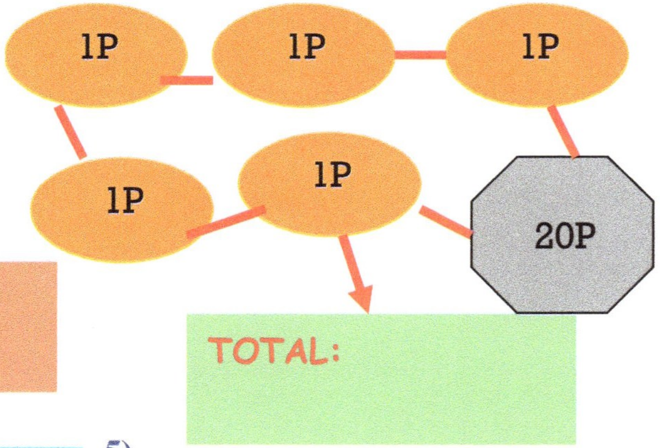

3) 5P, 5P, 5P, 5P, 5P, 20P, 20P — TOTAL:

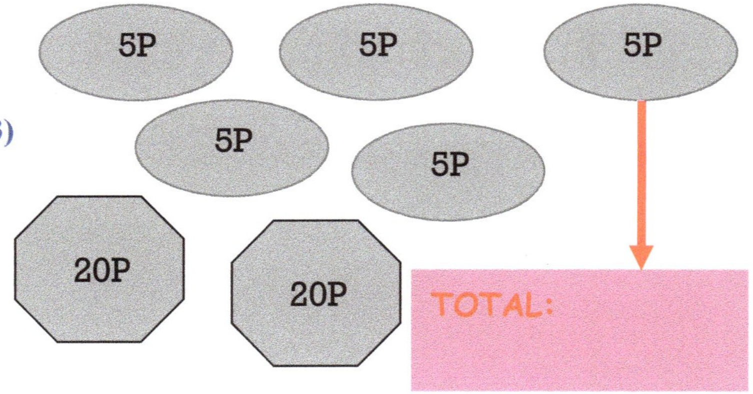

4) 50P, 50P, 50P, 2P, 2P — TOTAL:

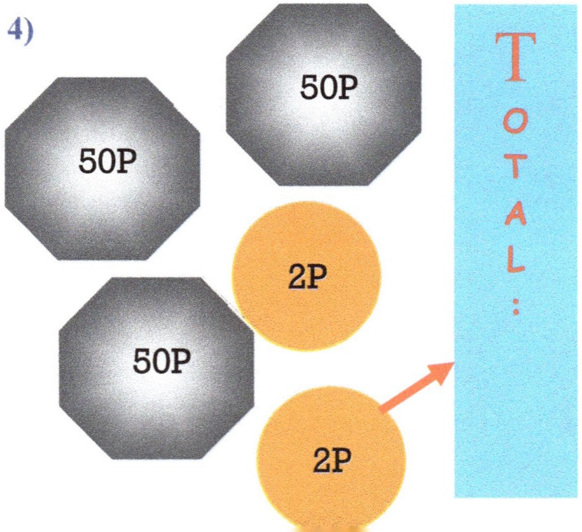

5) 50P, 20P, 5P, 10P, 2P, 1P, 1 Shape — TOTAL:

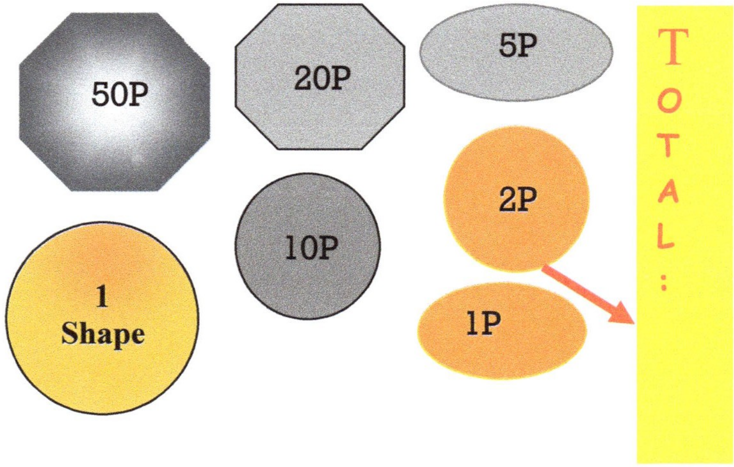

6) 20P, 2P, 50P, 1P — TOTAL:

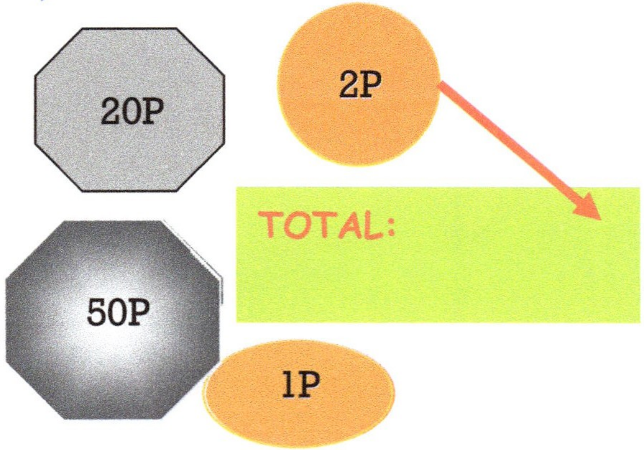

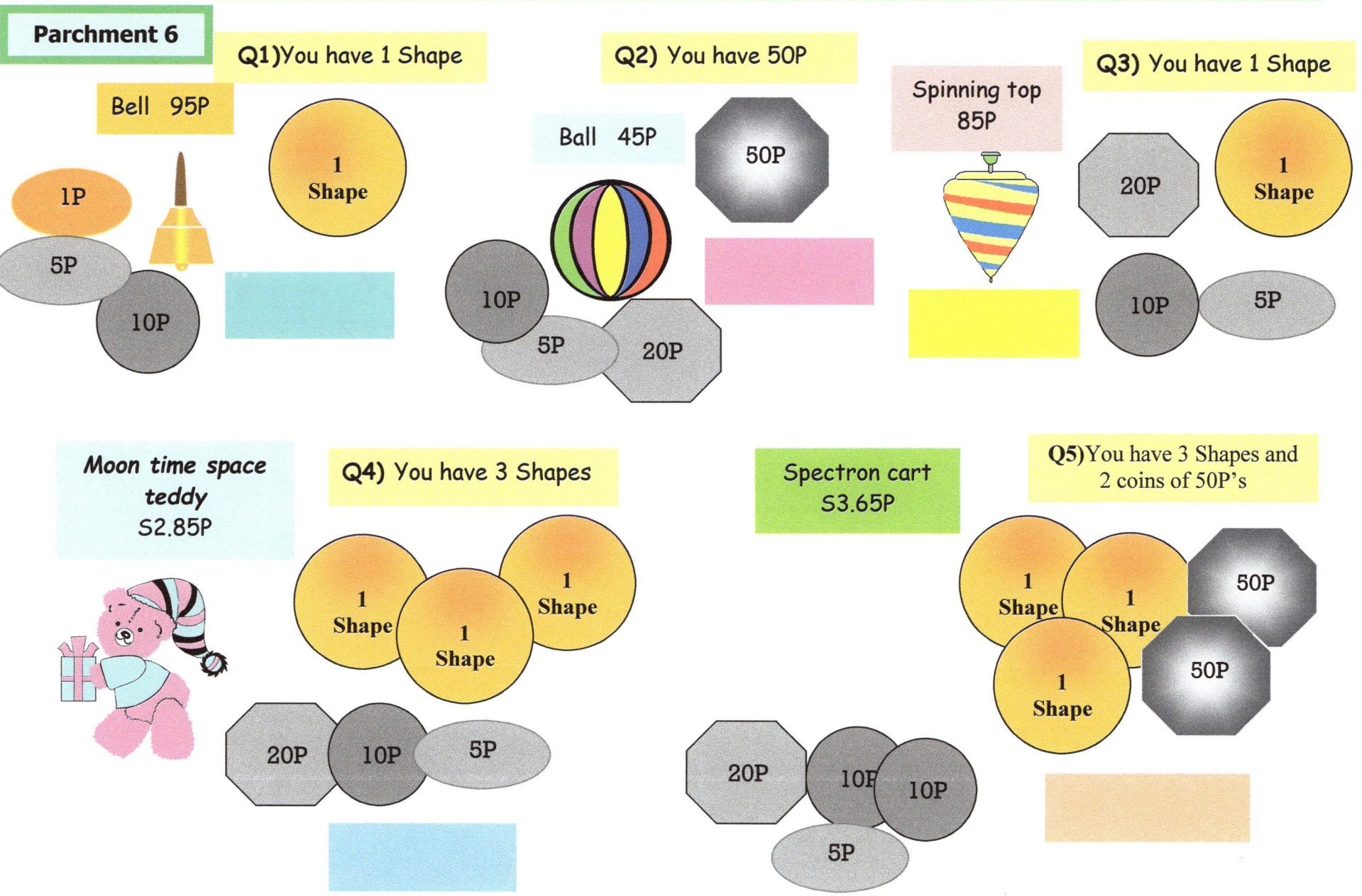

Tougher Lots of!

Parchment 7

Tricky!

Q 1)

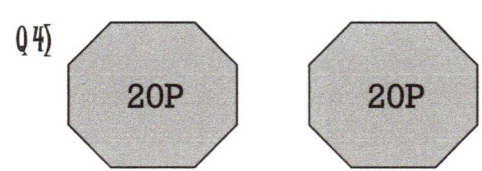

This coin is 50P or 50 Parts

We have 2 lots of 50 Parts here. **That means we have 100 Parts or a whole of a hundred**
2 coins X 50 Parts = 100 Parts
or

Q 4)

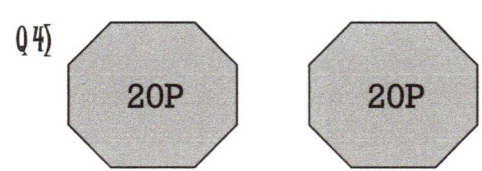

This coin is 20P or 20 Parts

This means we have 40 Parts. 2 coins X 20 Parts = 40 Parts. How many more coins would you need to make one Shape?

Q 2)

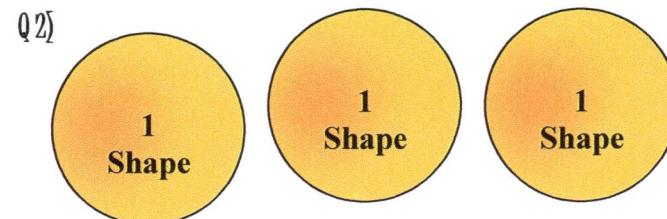

This coin is 100P or 100 Parts

We have 3 lots of 100 Parts here. How many parts would be in 3 Shapes?

Q 5)

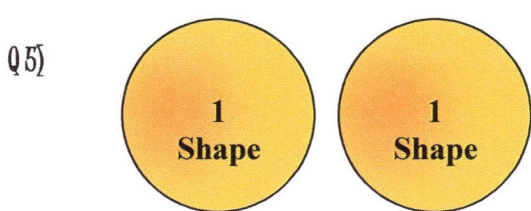

We have 2 Shapes here.
Remember, 1 Shape = 100 Parts

How many Parts do we have here altogether?

See if you can answer the questions below.

How many parts are in the coins? Tick the boxes.

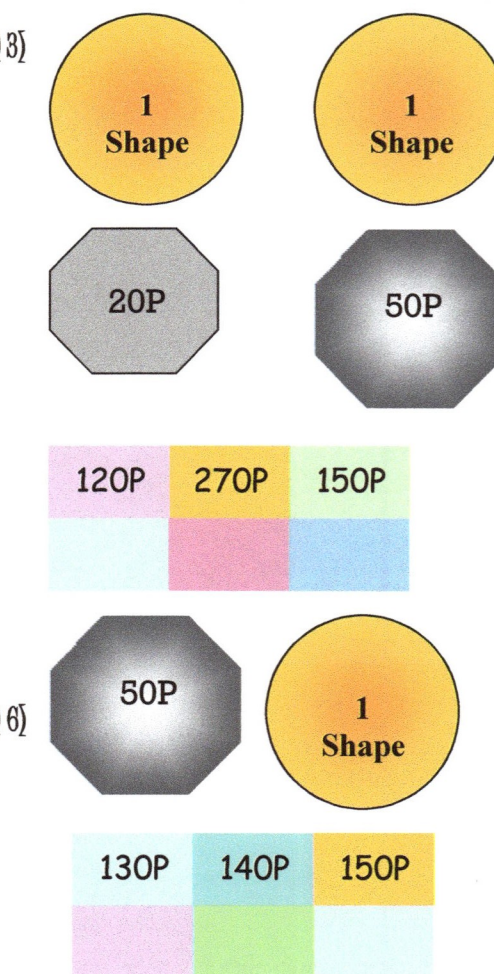

Parchment 9

Tougher questions – Remember, Will is working with Rupins and Pennies!

Will needs to know how much he earns each fortnight!

Will thinks, '10% is the easiest number to work out. If I earn 100 Rupins, I know that 10% of 100 is 10 Pennies.'

Will also knows that a percentage is a part of a quantity of 100!

3) If Will has 60 Rupins and puts 10% into his Savings and gives 10% to the Children's Home, how many Rupins will he have left?

1) Will knows the farmer has given him a 10% bonus for working hard. He has worked out that he has earned 60 Rupins for working the Saturdays and Sundays of two weekends. So if 10% of a 100 is 10, how much would 10% of 60 Rupins be?

Will was trying to work out this sum when he fell off his bike!

4) When it is very busy at the farm, Will has earned 100 Rupins, when he earns this amount of money, how much would 70% be?

2) Will's Special money is his living money and is usually 70% of the money he has earned while working for the farmer. If he has earned 60 Rupins, what would 70% of 60 Rupins be?

THINK!

Remember to divide 60 Rupins by 10 and then multiply by 7 this will help you to find your answer!

ANSWER SHEETS FOR PARCHMENTS

Parchment 1

Q 2) 24 legs
Q 3) 32 legs
Q 4) 40 legs
Q 5) 48 legs
Q 6) 56 legs

Parchment 2

Q 1) 4P or Parts
Q 2) 30P or Parts
Q 3) 59P or Parts

Parchment 3

Q 1) 60P or Parts
Q 2) 1 Shape & 20P or Parts
Q 3) 68P or Parts
Q 4) 30P or Parts
Q 5) 60P, 80P, 20P or Parts

Parchment 4

Drum: 50P + 20P + 5P

Ball: 2 X 20P + 5P

Doll: 50P + 2 X 20P + 5P

Lunar Cart: 1 Shape + 20P + 10P + 5P

Parchment 5

Q 1) 40P or Parts
Q 2) 25P or Parts
Q 3) 65P or Parts
Q 4) 1 Shape & 54P or Parts
Q 5) 1 Shape & 88P or Parts
Q 6) 73P or Parts

Parchment 6

Q 1) 5P or Parts
Q 2) 5P or Parts
Q 3) 10P + 5P making 15P or Parts
Q 4) 10P + 5P making 15P or Parts
Q 5) 20P + 10P + 5P making 35P or Parts

ANSWER SHEETS FOR PARCHMENTS

Parchment 7

Q 1) 1 Shape
Q 2) 300P or Parts
Q 3) 270P or Parts
Q 4) 3 X 20P or 60P or Parts
Q 5) 200P or Parts
Q 6) 150P or Parts

Parchment 8

Q 1) 20P + 10P + 5P = 35P

Q 2) 1 Shape + 50P + 10P + 20P + 5 + 20 + 5P
= 2 Shapes & 10P

Q 3) 1 Shape + 20P + 10P
= 1 Shape & 30P

Q 4) 50P + 20P + 10P + 2P + 1P
= 83P

Q 5) 6 X 1 Shape + 50P + 30P + 10P
= 6 Shapes & 90P

Q 6) 3 X 1 Shape + 2 X 20P + 5P
= 3 Shapes & 45P

Parchment 9

Q 1) 6 Rupins
Q 2) 42 Rupins
Q 3) 48 Rupins
Q 4) 70 Rupins

www.ingramcontent.com/pod-product-compliance
Lightning Source LLC
Chambersburg, PA
CBHW061537010526
44107CB00066B/2892